CREATE YOUR OWN FOOTBALL CLUB

CHAMPIONS EDITION

THIS BOOK BELONGS TO

....

Thank you for purchasing this book from amberoctopus, we hope you enjoy it.

Based in rural Buckinghamshire, amberoctopus is a small business created by a father of two young daughters. Our aim is to create engaging books for young people that spark their imagination and creativity – as well as giving parents a little break.

Please consider leaving a review on Amazon. This support will help us create more quality books in the future, thank you very much.

Visit **amberoctopus.com** for more information and to view our full range of books.

CONTENTS

There are three football clubs to complete. Each club has
16 tasks for you to design, colour and fill in the details.

1. CLUB BADGE
Design and colour the club badge

2. CLUB INFO
Complete all the club information

3. HOME KIT
Design and colour the home kit

4. AWAY KIT
Design and colour the away kit

5. KEEPER KIT
Design and colour the goalkeeper kit

6. SQUAD
Complete the squad list

7. STARTING 11
Decide who makes the starting lineup

8. MANAGER
Colour the manager

9. CAPTAIN CARD
Complete the captain's stats card

10. STADIUM
Colour the club's stadium

11. TROPHIES
Colour and name the trophies

12. TRAINING KIT
Design and colour the training kit

13. MERCHANDISE
Design and colour fan merchandise

14. FLAG
Design a flag for supporters

15. TICKETS
Complete the matchday ticket

16. PROGRAMME
Combine your previous designs to create a matchday programme

FOOTBALL CLUB

1

1. CLUB BADGE

2. CLUB INFO

CLUB NAME: ....
FOUNDED: ....
LEAGUE: ....
NICKNAME: ....
STADIUM: ....
CAPACITY: ....
OWNERS: ....
CHAIRMAN: ....
MANAGER: ....

LEAGUE TITLES: ....
DOMESTIC CUPS: ....
CONTINENTAL CUPS: ....

MOST APPEARANCES: ....
RECORD GOALSCORER: ....
RECORD SIGNING: ....

4. AWAY KIT

GOALKEEPERS

Number	Name	Number	Name
....	....	....	....
....	....	....	....

DEFENDERS

Number	Name	Number	Name
....	....	....	....
....	....	....	....
....	....	....	....
....	....	....	....

MIDFIELDERS

Number	Name	Number	Name
....	....	....	....
....	....	....	....
....	....	....	....
....	....	....	....

FORWARDS

Number	Name	Number	Name
....	....	....	....
....	....	....	....
....	....	....	....

6. SQUAD

7. STARTING 11

9. CAPTAIN CARD

Rating

Position

National flag

Name

Shooting

Dribbling

Passing

Tackling

Pace

Strength

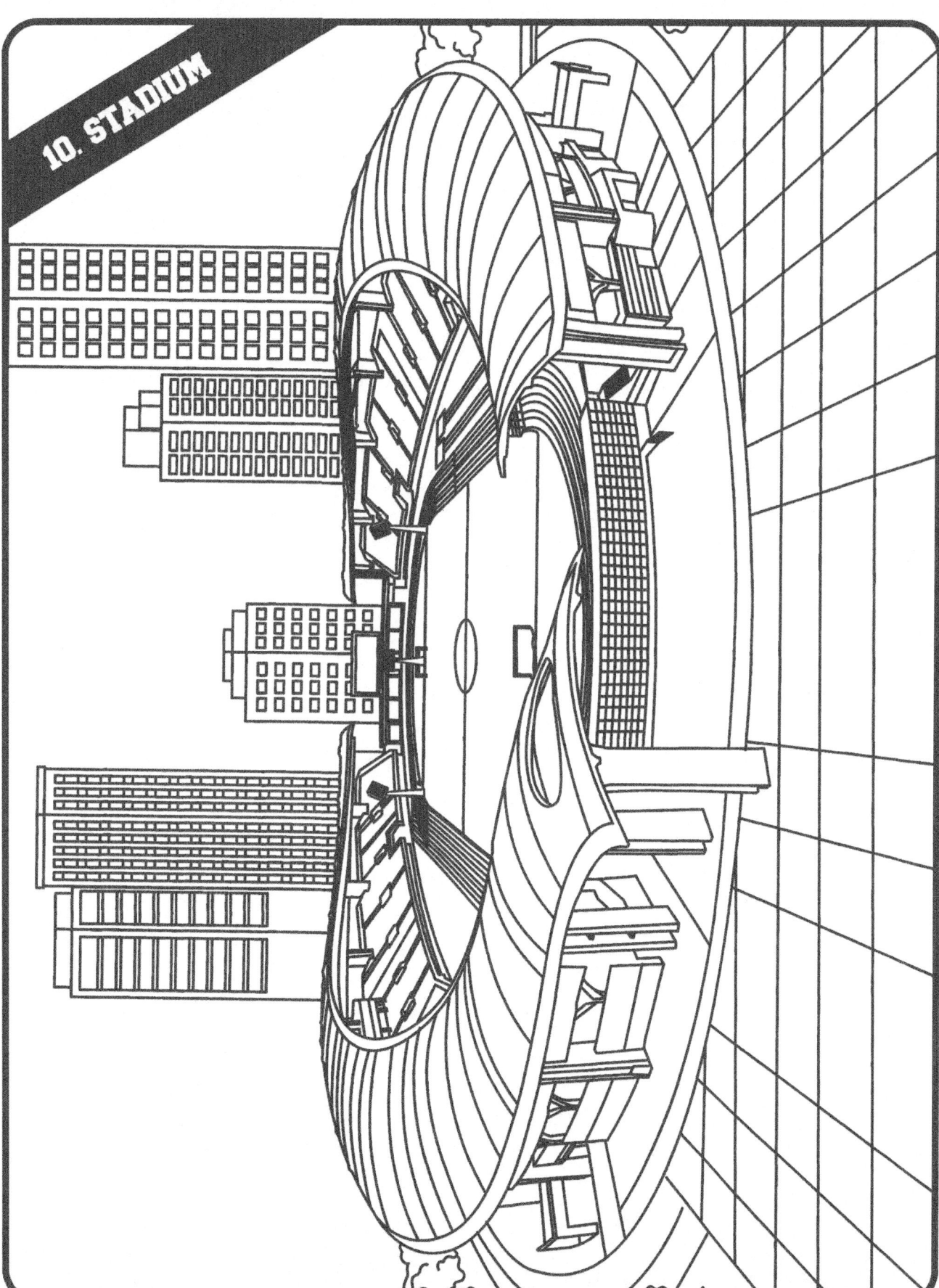

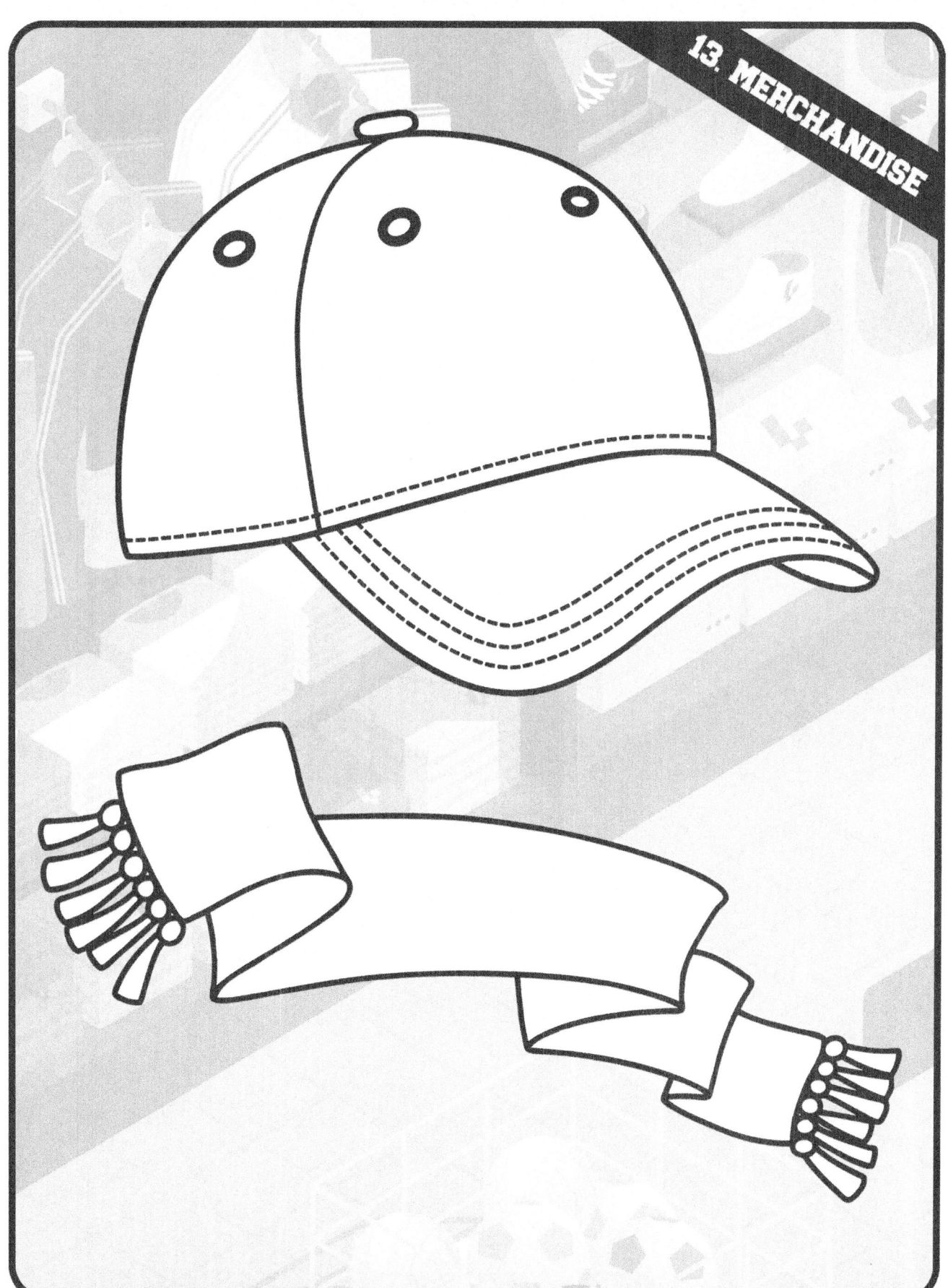

14. FLAG

15. TICKETS

OFFICIAL MATCHDAY PROGRAMME

16. PROGRAMME

VS. _____

VENUE:
DATE:
KICK OFF:

ISSUE 1
£

LEAGUE LOGO

CLUB SPONSORS

FOOTBALL CLUB

2

1. CLUB BADGE

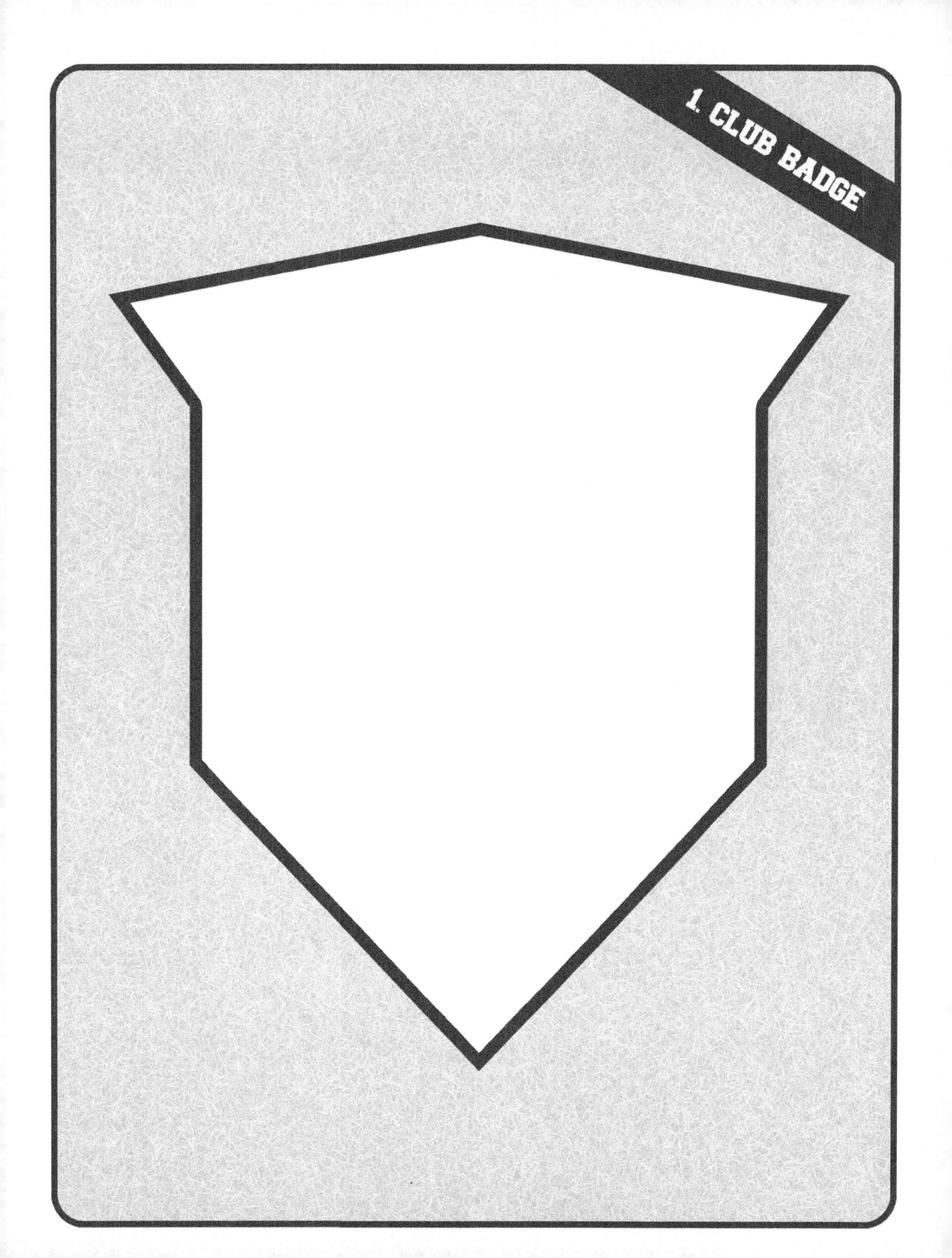

2. CLUB INFO

CLUB NAME : ....

FOUNDED : ....

LEAGUE : ....

NICKNAME : ....

STADIUM : ....

CAPACITY : ....

OWNERS : ....

CHAIRMAN : ....

MANAGER : ....

LEAGUE TITLES : ....

DOMESTIC CUPS : ....

CONTINENTAL CUPS : ....

MOST APPEARANCES : ....

RECORD GOALSCORER : ....

RECORD SIGNING : ....

3. HOME KIT

4. AWAY KIT

5. KEEPER KIT

GOALKEEPERS

Number	Name	Number	Name
....	....	....	....
....	....	....	....

DEFENDERS

Number	Name	Number	Name
....	....	....	....
....	....	....	....
....	....	....	....
....	....	....	....

MIDFIELDERS

Number	Name	Number	Name
....	....	....	....
....	....	....	....
....	....	....	....
....	....	....	....

FORWARDS

Number	Name	Number	Name
....	....	....	....
....	....	....	....
....	....	....	....

6. SQUAD

7. STARTING 11

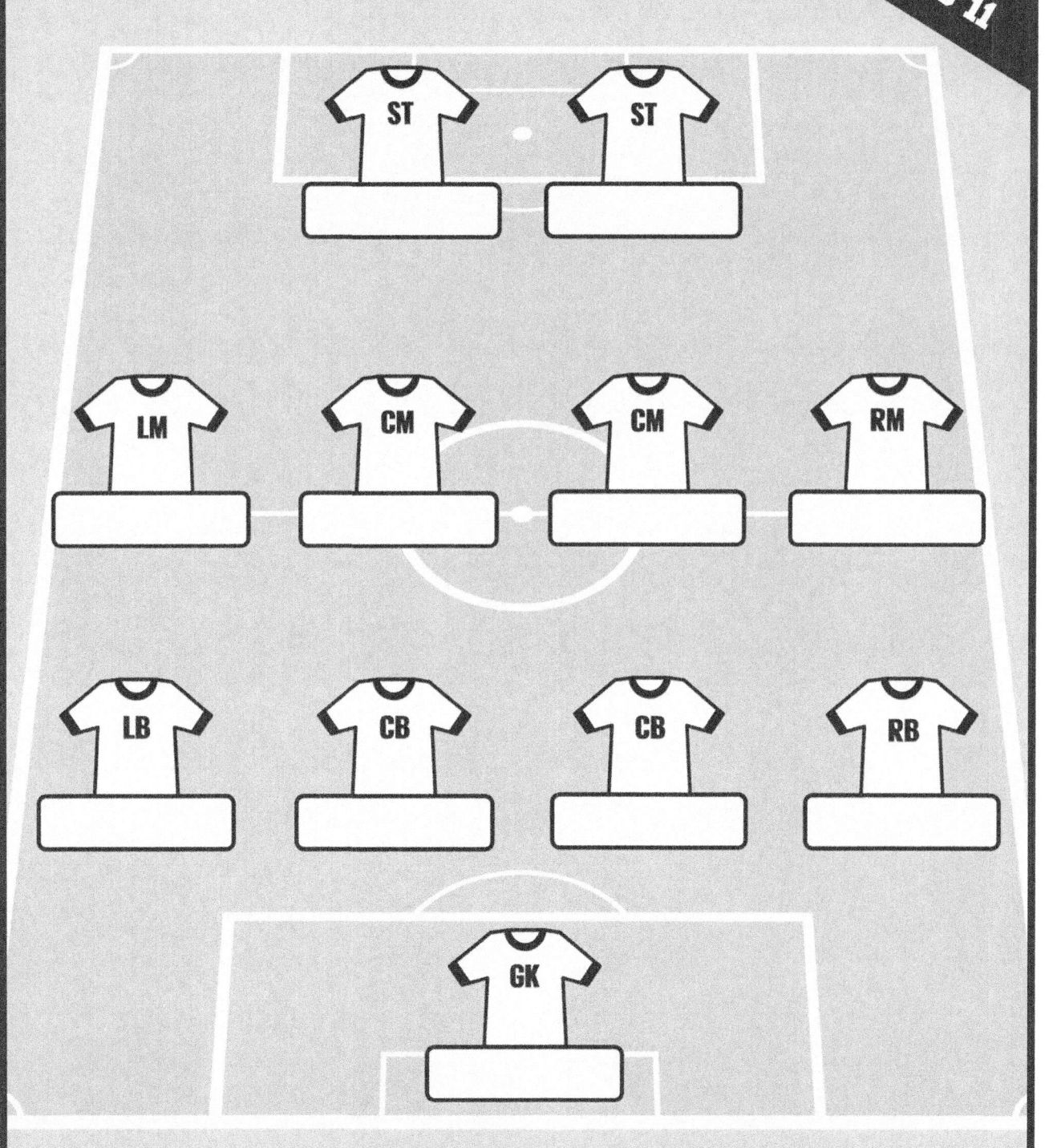

8. MANAGER

9. CAPTAIN CARD

Rating

Position

National flag

Name

Shooting

Passing

Pace

Dribbling

Tackling

Strength

10. STADIUM

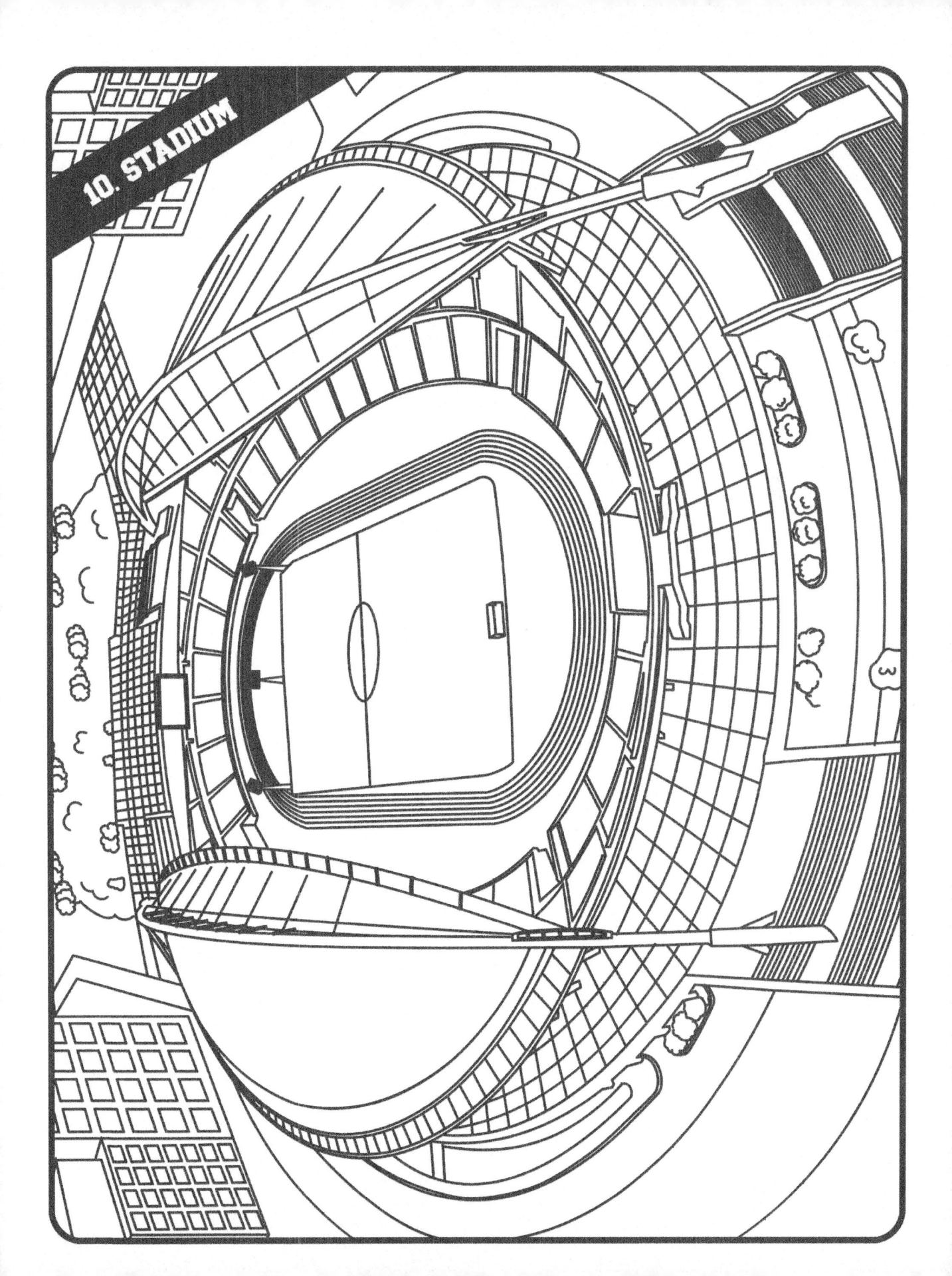

11. TROPHIES

12. TRAINING KIT

13. MERCHANDISE

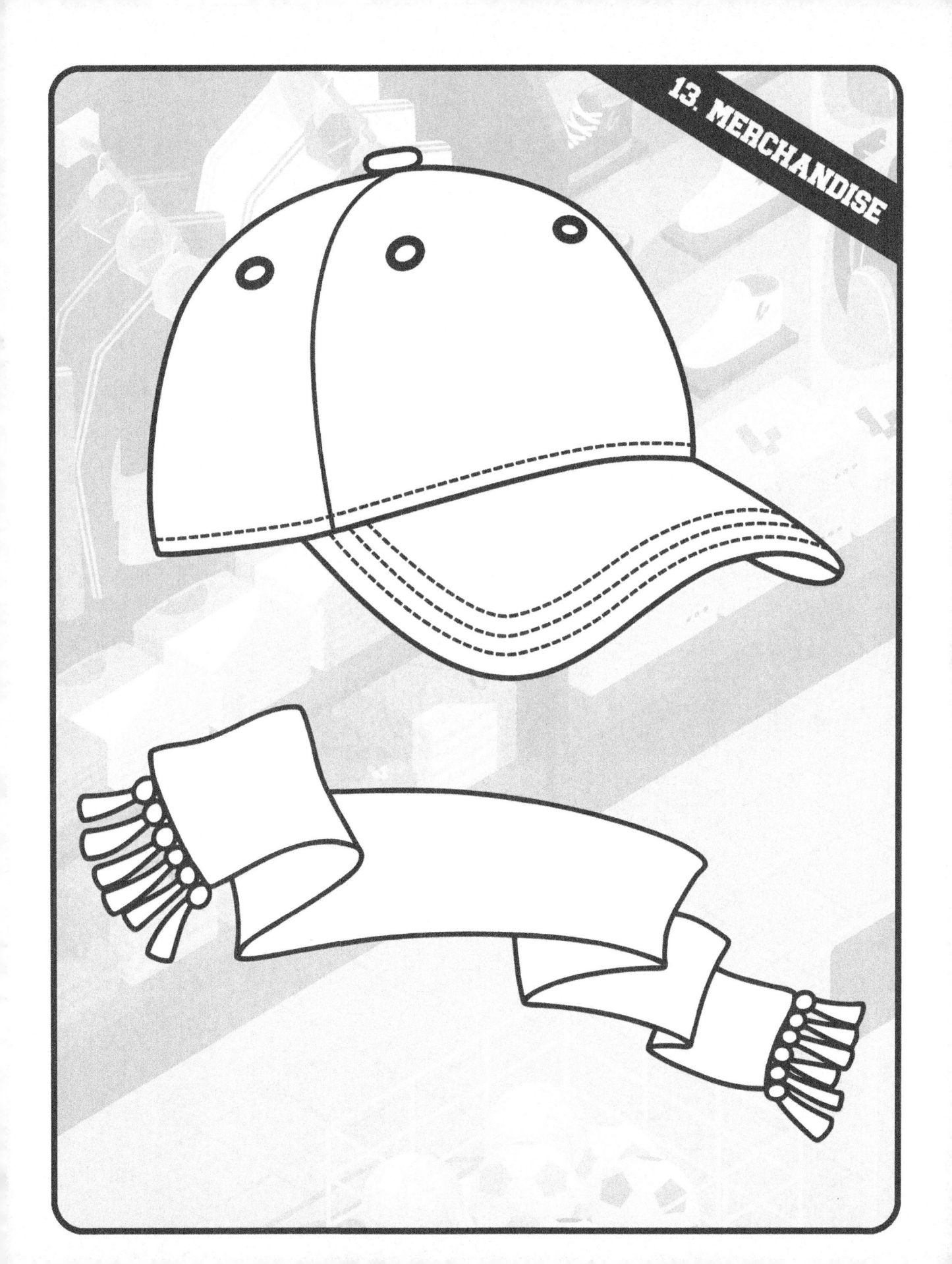

14. FLAG

15. TICKETS

MATCH DATE	___/___/___

_____ VS. _____

VENUE _____
STAND _____
PRICE _____

CLUB BOX OFFICE
Website:
Telephone:

TICKET NUMBER: _____
COMPETITION _____

MATCHDAY SPONSORS

GATE	ROW	SEAT

OFFICIAL MATCHDAY PROGRAMME

16. PROGRAMME

VS. _____

VENUE:
DATE:
KICK OFF:

ISSUE 1
£

LEAGUE LOGO

CLUB SPONSORS

FOOTBALL CLUB

3

1. CLUB BADGE

2. CLUB INFO

CLUB NAME : ....

FOUNDED : ....

LEAGUE : ....

NICKNAME : ....

STADIUM : ....

CAPACITY : ....

OWNERS : ....

CHAIRMAN : ....

MANAGER : ....

LEAGUE TITLES : ....

DOMESTIC CUPS : ....

CONTINENTAL CUPS : ....

MOST APPEARANCES : ....

RECORD GOALSCORER : ....

RECORD SIGNING : ....

3. HOME KIT

4. AWAY KIT

5. KEEPER KIT

GOALKEEPERS

Number	Name	Number	Name
....	....	....	....
....	....	....	....

DEFENDERS

Number	Name	Number	Name
....	....	....	....
....	....	....	....
....	....	....	....
....	....	....	....

MIDFIELDERS

Number	Name	Number	Name
....	....	....	....
....	....	....	....
....	....	....	....
....	....	....	....

FORWARDS

Number	Name	Number	Name
....	....	....	....
....	....	....	....
....	....	....	....

6. SQUAD

7. STARTING 11

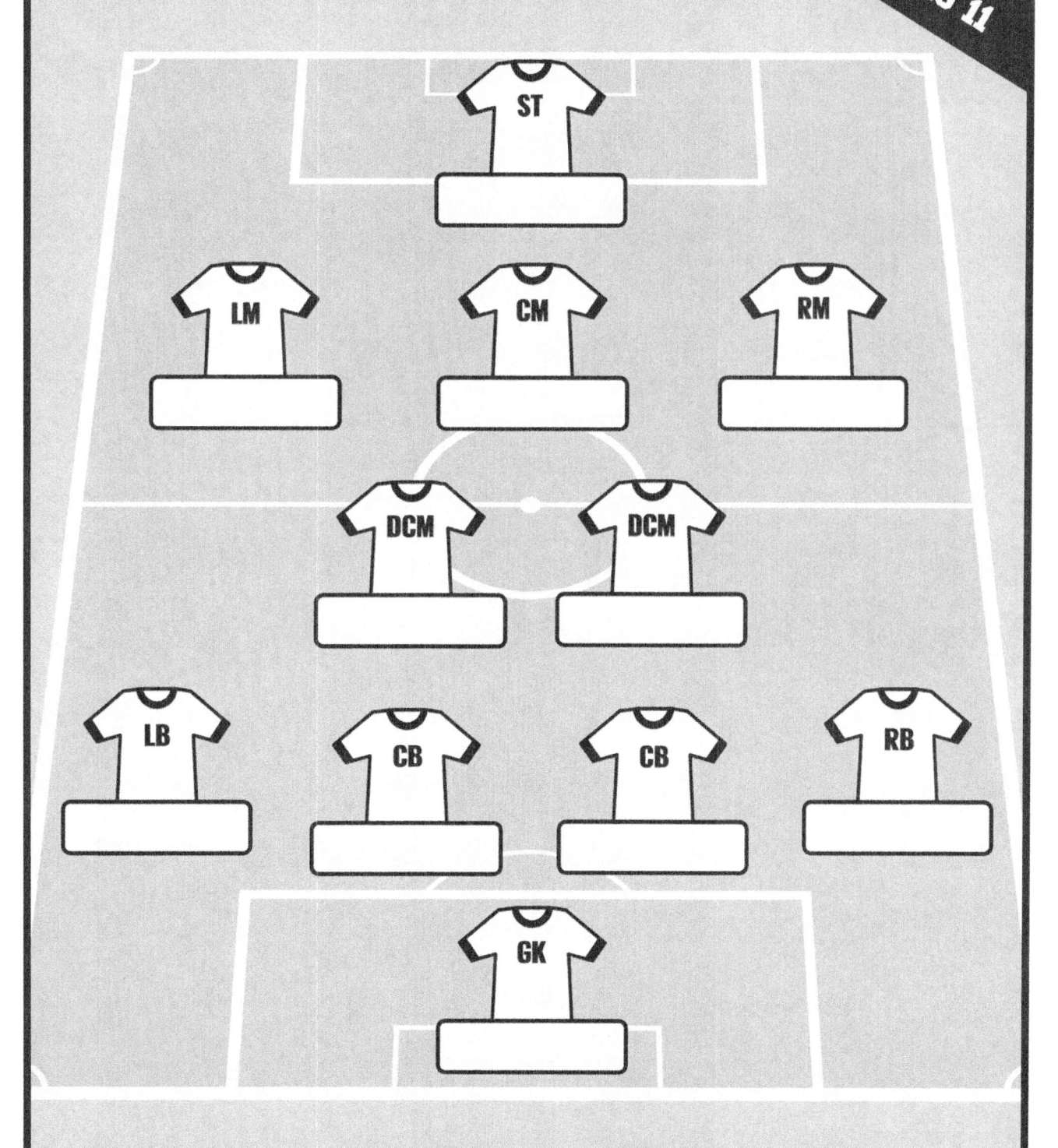

8. MANAGER

9. CAPTAIN CARD

Rating

Position

National flag

Name

Shooting

Dribbling

Passing

Tackling

Pace

Strength

10. STADIUM

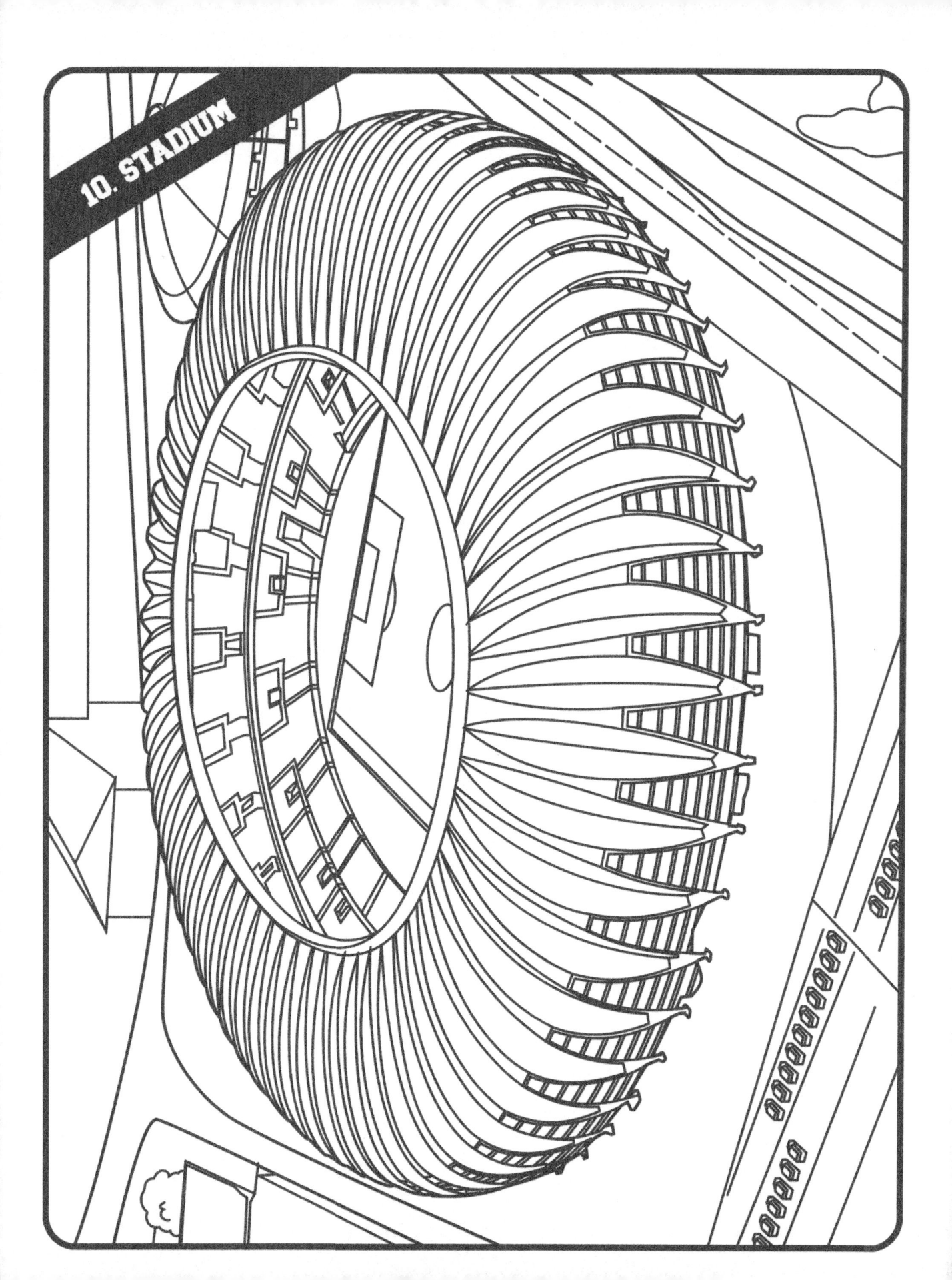

11. TROPHIES

12. TRAINING KIT

13. MERCHANDISE

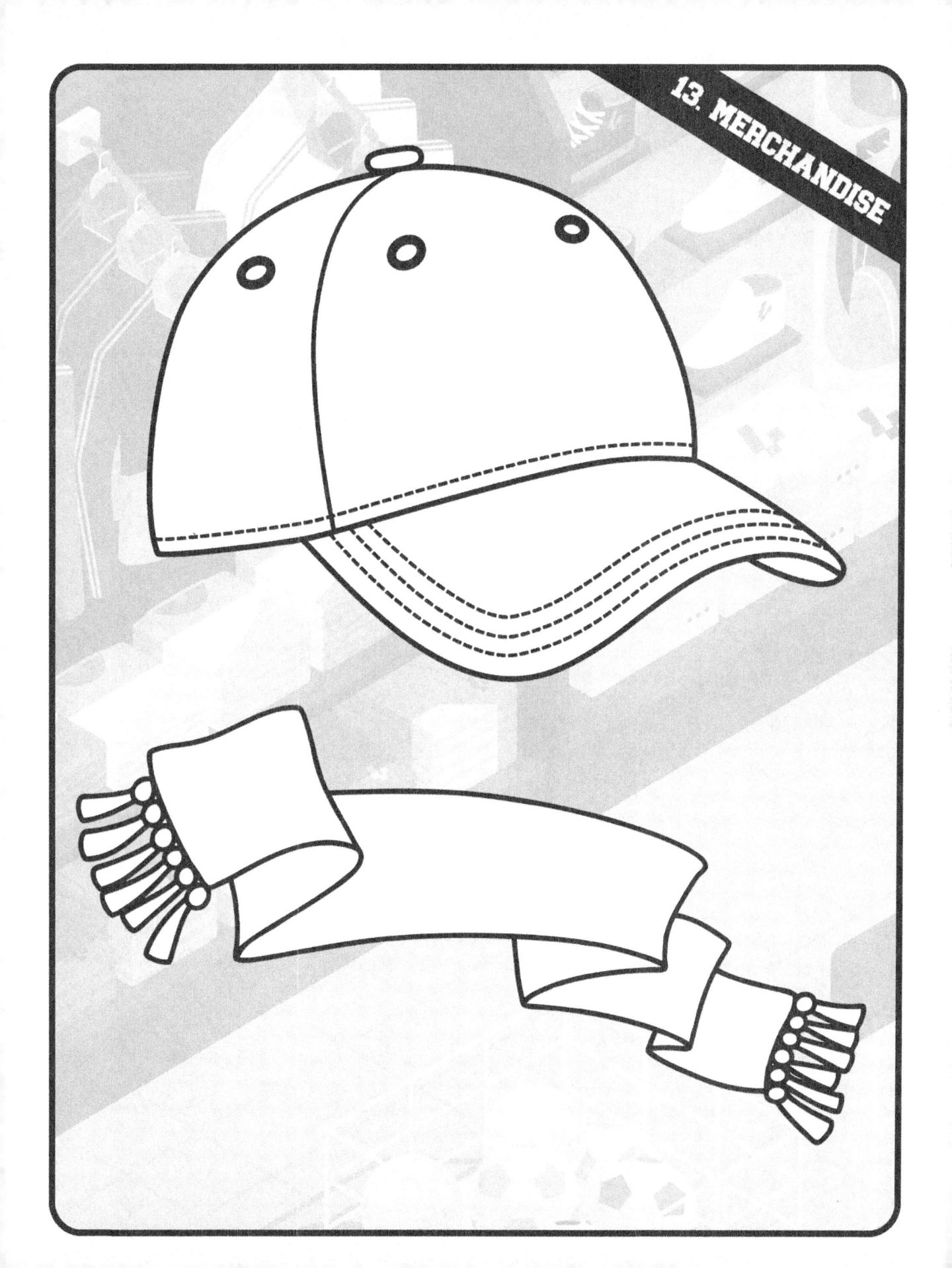

14. FLAG

15. TICKETS

OFFICIAL MATCHDAY PROGRAMME

16. PROGRAMME

VS. _____

VENUE:
DATE:
KICK OFF:

ISSUE 1
£

LEAGUE LOGO

CLUB SPONSORS

Printed in Great Britain
by Amazon